Fresh Window

Poems
(1980)

Michael Cooper

edited by Gerard Malanga

SPUYTEN DUYVIL
New York City

ISBN 978-1-963908-00-8

Library of Congress Control Number: 2024939704

I very much enjoyed and admired these poems—for their delicacy and tenderness, for the way they evoke the mutual permeability of person and world and person and person, for the delicate balance they strike between occlusion and transparency of vision. They remind me of Frank O'Hara's lovers "drifting back and forth/ between each other like a tree breathing through its spectacles . . ." Thank you for entrusting me with them.
    Ellen Levy

Michael Cooper is the poet of the little epiphanies of everyday life—a sensitive person who can find importance and beauty in what sometimes might seem mundane. Michael is not afraid to delve into sexuality, and often writes rather detailed poetry that mirrors the feelings and behavior of physical love. This is genuine poetry, but rarely obscure. This doesn't mean it's simple, or perhaps superficial. What he has revealed to me is only a small amount of what seems like a lifetime of writing and contemplating reality with a poet's eye. A wonderful romp through the need for poetry and the awareness of its potential and limitations, Cooper has hit just the right balance between a reality that might appear trivial and a perception of how any reality can contain revelations.
    John Wherrity

I am eager to express my astonishment at Cooper's sensibility and love of language. Also his determination to see, feel, to squeeze, report, to blend, delve, to do all those things that celebrate noticing. I relish the bite and theology of a piece like "The Man Who Got Arrested for Impersonating the Deity." I thought I was reading Frost!
    Paul Bernabeo

for my Mother

CONTENTS

PART I

PART II

PART III

PART IV

PART I

TUESDAY

I keep thinking it's Thursday
when it's Wednesday.

PICTURE OF GANDHI

A man carries his boots home
under an umbrella when it's
raining.

NOVEL

I look in the mirror to see if
my face is still there. I want to
write a decadent novel, but don't.

DUCKING

It looks like this white
is a physical thing,
and it's ducking
under it.

CONTRACTIONS

The bricks on the sidewalk:
a green truck pulls over them.
A man bangs a broom:
I cannot hear the sound.

HOUSE IN CONNECTICUT

He advanced boldly toward the
                              mechanism.

The lampposts in New York
are taller than the houses
in most cities.

WITH REFERENCE TO ROOSEVELT

How a flute sounds like a viola
when a printing press is
running in the basement.

He hears the radio through the sound
                    of the machine,
the obscure "he" that is himself.

"See my watch? See my entrails?"

PINK

Sky is ice:
a last crash
before the floor collapses.
Drink the glass
that spreads out
into puddles
of thin meaning.
You ask for flowers,
returning the captives
of density
to their lawful
walks of life.
The pink concrete
that no one
lets go of.

FACE

The entrance of deception
is a crust on top of bread,
because of flatulence
wherever birds are scorned.
The obvious encouragement
that hair provides the head,
like a train to Astoria.
You're the one that pulls
the weeds in my garden.
The discrete whistling of
the fan that needs oiling.
There is no time to read.

SLICKER

A man waves to a taxi as to an old friend.
He says, "Hello! Remember me?"
The car drives on ahead, and passes him.
Across the rainy street,
the white lines, freshly painted,
stand out against the black.
Two musicians switch guitars.
A little boy in a yellow raincoat
with a green umbrella
walks home with his mother.

DE KOONING

The flight of gulls is impaired
by sparrows that cross their path,
and owls who wander 'round
the periphery of the circle they trace,
wherein we wait for summer's end.

I live beyond the tornado:
the crusted field that is spread
across with sawdust.
Splinters fall beneath my foot,
which tests the solidity of snow.

MILLIONS OF WHITE SHIRTS

Glimmering in the sunshine.

DO I STAND

Am I standing between you and the landscape,
like a tree between your vision and the sky,
or the lake, so blue in the evening sun?

CUPS SHOES ALIVE WET AND WATERLILIES

That's why I like the mug you bought me:
The impression of trees in the distance
    image
    idea

feathery branches black against
    a brown horizon.

MOON

I don't know how many times

I've mistaken for the moon,

The reflection in my window

Of a lightbulb in the room.

POEM

Five eggplants on the sidewalk
by the fence along the
cemetery's edge at midnight,
as the wind
blows through the branches
of trees whose limbs
hang over from among
the tombstones where they grow,
scattering leaves to the ground.

LEAVES

It had turned so suddenly cold.
Summer was over. Time to hang up leaves
on the wall when they fall to the floor.
Sheets of paper from a notebook.

PART II

KILTER

The park is vacant. The church's
towers loom above the tree, like
taller trees, or mountain tops.
No one comes here anymore. There
is a fear of sudden cold: the
snow that must come soon. What if
the weather is as responsive to
our changing moods as we are to it?
The time is out of kilter, and
one doesn't know what makes things
fit. The sparrows flutter in the
dirt, pressing themselves into it,
wings flapping.

NARCISSUS IN A GARDEN

Because the light is soft,
the train is quiet. Sleeping bodies,
still persons in some sense,
obscured from consciousness
by the subtle, padded coating
which disguises the obscurity
of their destination: coalmines,
clavichords, Narcissus in
a garden, the vast and
tightly braided golden hair
that means, somehow, existence
is in progress, and somehow,
not yet complete, the faces'
features cannot be distinguished.
This moves us through the night,
as limp limbs fall back into
stagnant lack of memory.
We plunge into this pool that
is unconsciousness, or the lack
of anything worth focusing on.
Forgetful of our past, the

singularity of the moment
ceases to be cogent. I think
of you, not sure exactly what, or
who you are, but knowing, or
rather, at least sensing, some-
where you exist—   I reach
out, stretching memory's grasp,
my fingers clasping hold
of anything to start with, some
connective to begin and then
go on with, an unobtrusive con-
stant, something like the
sun, or stars in general, the
specific that reflects and yet
contains the vaster whole. The
conductor rushes down the
aisle with a flashlight.

THE DAYS

This floating resonance
is an evocation of you
among the surly memories
of wooden forests:
there is a flavor
of moss in my mouth.
Conduits, like stanzas,
convey my thoughts
like water from
my mind to my hand,
and you are there:
the completion of syntax
that receives me, and
alleviates what would
have been my fate:
a suspended sentence.
We ride now, on the
top of a double-decker
bus: the sun
beats down on our heads.
You have succeeded

in continuing to
smile in the face
of a cloudless sky.
I have received notice
of your recent consecration.
The world is overwhelmed,
and as we sip our tea,
together, we wonder as one mind:
Do the artifices we've built up
warrant the continuance of
our attentions?
Slow cracks in the pavement
move, containing stones that
fall beneath our feet.
The emptiness of winter
is upon us. The days
are getting shorter.

THE PARTHENON IN RAIN

Because the light glows inside your eyes
which teach me the lessons that the night
has to offer, we are of one mind,
and in accordance with our natures,

descend into obeisance to our instincts.
We are thrust out of that peace which we
had forfeited upon surrender to ourselves.
Your nature once again holds me accountable:

I step outside and watch the doors,
opening and closing. The train reverses
itself, and something has been settled.
The pen leaves my hand for an instant,

and returns. The farm in Pennsylvania;
the cows on the lawn. An expression
of gratitude: a substitute of words.
Two nurses play magnetic backgammon.

I place my cufflinks through the holes,
fastening them on the other side.
The Polish immigrant.
The stadium casts an eery light.

I am left with a sense of being restored.
There is a telephone at home tonight.
The way the machine grips the paper
out of your hand: the dock-feed

through which it passes to the other side,
taking it into itself. Trying not to exhibit
too much enthusiasm, he doesn't say much.
Knowing they would be there, he was

prepared from the start for umbrellas,
cantaloupes, the Parthenon in rain.
You reach through it, fingers clutching
air; air that reaches back into itself.

The enemy moves slowly through the desert,
like a camel, lacking water,
and will go further than anyone
might think. He disregards advertisements,

because the air has gotten suddenly cold.
The day was successful, in that he arrived
home safely once again, or was about to.
He did not see the picture show, but

watched the moving scenery rush by
through the window of a train at night,
recreating something of a similar sensation.
He did not eat noodles, but meat, instead.

He did not walk through an airline terminal,
but through a subway station. The people
did not speak quietly to one another, but
loudly, as though unconscious of where they were.

She rode her bicycle home through the misty rain.

ROSE

I.

In what would seem to be a pause
to relieve the tension caused by
constant occupation, the dissat-
isfaction in the moment expanded
into panic at the lack of a hair-
cut, which could not be had, be-
cause there was no mirror through
which to see behind oneself. The
air was stagnant; the impending
thunderstorm sublimated into hum-
idity. He turned inwards, revers-
ing an impulse to deal outwardly
with an image of the invisible.
Retrieving a sense of wholeness,
or attempting to, the windows
opened, rivers flowing downstream.
"Unfurl thy furrowed brow," he
said to her that evening; an im-
perative to prompt the frighten-
ed gardens from exploding in

                                        the heat. This new arbor, roses
growing near the house, a fine
example of her delicate tendency
to read through bricks, the pale
pink skin that, suddenly exposed
to air, trembled slightly, the
subtlest change of temperature,
rendered her an umbrella, left
in a room, when it was not rain-
ing. The telephone waited by his
side, and occasionally his elbow
would feel its calm and plastic
touch. The day being clear, and
then a moment later, threaten-
ingly dark, he went indoors and
remained there, having nothing
better to do. The clock progress-
ed; all those domestic moments,
like books on a shelf. What was
it all but waiting?; so many
people, not at home. When would
they all return? Questions, like
seconds; seconds, like similes;
his mind was a sea, a clutter of
nonsense. He strove to relate

them: tattered bits of cloth.
Then, dinner in the garden. The
quiet sounds of eating; tinkling
of glasses; soft conversation;
he was miserable. No, he would
not dress for dinner, not tonight.

II.

The sun rose early that morning.
He found her by the window,
with a young sparrow in her hand.
Her tenderness was moving.

UMBRELLA

When I rolled up the rug,
the perpendicular orifice which remained
resembled my heart:
an umbrella left inside the house.
The Grandmother, who
would not let me leave if I went in
again to get it: you
go for me. The straw mat
is all unrolled, now as we had
hidden it safely under
the steps. The construction
is awkward, and inverted.
The paper bleeds to the edge
where the print falls off,
like where the world ends:
that place at the end
of it. The table is flat,
but its angle betrays a strange
perspective: the painting that
is not the world, but a
representation of it. The boy
who wrote the word "blue,"

meaning "The fuse blew out," in
a Mother's Day letter
to his mother. They say the
horizon (where the ocean meets
the sky) is horizontal, from wherever
it is viewed.
The trees on the lawn reach up
to the windows. She makes a couple of
hamburgers for supper.

SHRUBBERY

Here, in the morning, the vestibule-like
protuberance causes him to open the afternoon
window: the crickets chirping on the lawn
and in the shrubbery that lines
the roadside. A little boy runs under
a tree: he's looking for something.
This September sun shines intently down
on the clay-like color of the cedar chips
that are really earth or bricks
through a wire-mesh screen when the
vision is blurred. The suburban sounds
are habitual: no one notices
mopeds, lawnmowers, airplanes.
A tree moves its leaves, consciously.
The shadows mirror a non-physical reality
that approximates an image without
its inherent virtue.

THE MEMORY OF GLOVES

One must have the strength to pour the tea,
which the waves in air make every
effort to prevent one from doing.
The simple gestures that give space
                              a meaning
define the limitations
within which one exists—
The sounds that greet the ear
                    in desperation——
The sudden absence of sound
among antiques in cabinets-—
The distant whirring of the
smooth machinery of night
that runs in a box
in the corner of the world, somewhere,
forgotten.

The memory of gloves.

WATER

A certain casual elegance
of things the way they are
on a day when it is
going to rain and one
wants to wear a raincoat
although it is too hot to,
there is still something
comforting about it.
One puts it on one's shoulders
and reclaims an old allegiance
of a gray New York day,
when one wants to wander
in the rain, and the non-rain
that is not only the absence
of rain: it is the vacancy
of mind that reflects
the blankness of the page
on which one is writing.
The emptiness fills up again:
A glass of water swallowed whole.

FRESH WINDOW

The man whistles and the dog
runs out the door.
The door is open and
it is a summer afternoon.
The dog comes into the store.
Who is saying this?
Who sees the door come
into the store and run
out again?
The dog whistles and
the man comes into the store.
The door is open
and it is a lovely
summer afternoon.
I'm thinking of a beautiful girl,
and the dog runs out the door.
It is a beautiful sunny day,
and a girl is in my mind.
I feel like a summer afternoon
when I kiss her and she smiles.
When she laughs she giggles.

A dog walks in the door
and runs out again.
A girl walks through the door
and a man becomes a boy,
and the girl becomes a woman.
The dog has gone away,
and someone is heard
whistling in the distance.

PART III

PART II

DOORKNOB

It's the shovel:
the song of the wayfarer
in harmony with the doorknob.
They are centipedes in
the wilderness. The grain
of wood on the broomstick
is exposed by the paint
which has eroded.
There she is. The red
handle like a wishbone
by the seaside.

FALL IN MY SHOE

STROPHE

My cat sits on my lap,
snowy white like a chicken:
I stroke her feathers.

If it were not for the paws
and tail hanging down,
the sensation would be identical.

ANTISTROPHE

My cat sat on my lap,
white like a chicken:
I stroked her feathers.

If it had not been for the paws
and tail hanging down
that moved of its own accord,

the sensation would have been identical.

ALMOST AFTERNOON

In the soft light of morning,
which is partially from an electric lamp,
because there is no window where there is supposed to be,
I cut the grapefruit into sections and eat it.
Rachmaninoff's saxophone on the radio
plays Symphonic Dances from Huntington, Long Island,
like Milhaud's Creation of The World for a moment.
The toast is in the oven, burning.

NOT QUITE A SONNET

Now that the world has come and gone again,
Snowplows drive down a street devoid of snow.
And when the world awakes at night again,
The store with all the lights in the window
Opens up its doors and the sky is blue.
When yesterday we heard the ringing bells,
A horse-drawn sleigh went up the street at noon.
A blue candle melted without a smell.

SHORT BLUE SLIPS

I love to go to the bathroom,
and stay there,
in the dark warm place
with the lights out
and the radiator on,
and sit there;
my head in my hands,
thinking of trees and
summer mornings.
And no one is there,
and no one speaks.
I listen only
for the sound
of the doorknob,
turning.

EATING YOUR LASAGNA

This research I am engaged in
(an inquiry into your desperate intelligence),
sustains me through a meal,
and, like a meal (which in fact it is),
my thoughts are focused on lasagna,
which evokes a sensation of you.

Eating your lasagna,
you merge into the experience of it.
I see you as one visual plane
with the wall behind you;
no sense of perspective.
The noodles are soft:
the ripples in their edges, sensuous.

Looking across the table at you,
I see you, flat against the wall.
Ingesting noodles, you pick them up
with your fork from the plate
on the table in front of you,
before you eat them.

I see you as one with your surroundings:
a personal presence that
defines the situation.
You exist within it, as the
noodles become part of you.
An intimate occurance;
a process which becomes made known,
or visible, as the eye discerns,
and gradually perceives the image.

The lasagna is a pretext,
a prerequisite to anything:
the necessity that protrudes
beyond itself.

The eye frames a picture
of what is in front of it.
An interior landscape:
the surface of the table,
the objects on it, the wall
behind you, and you among it.
A still life: the camera does not move.

The situation exists purely
in the relation of its elements.
The lasagna is the activator,
the lithe connective that sets
the scene in motion.
If it were not for the wall . . .

PART IV

ORIFICE

Stumbling, like an elixir
dissolving cataracts,
the Eggplant Inventor
of the Roof experiences
a genuine cry of terror,
as he enters a region
inaccessible beforehand.
Catching wind of a
passing apparition,
you cascade into my hands,
where you are cradled,
like a slight moon in the
sky. As I offer you
my coach to see you home,
the door is opened, and
we climb the stairs.
The stars are out, although
we cannot see them for
the mist that's risen. You
suddenly become realistic:
a mirror with the fog wiped away.

SAUCER

This saucer full of twilight,
where the window
meets the outside world:
I see the slight world
billowing in pain: a cloud
that floats, heavy, before
the rain. The train rides
up into the night-blackening
sky: my eye sees through
the glass. The foreseeable
future marches in a line
across the plain, like snow-
drifts. The dark stain of
night, blood-red on white
sheets that cover me: my
body that waits for
morning, which does not come.

NEWFOUNDLAND

So they go through you. The hair
on women's legs. The trees in the
forest. Crowded aisles. Singing
boys in their deafness. The
terrible French ocean that speaks
in your sleep. They are returning.
The moon will never be the same.
I will thank you for the likeness
of your life that you exposed me
to sometime. The telephone poles
that populate the fields,
laced through with railroad
tracks. Captivated by our image
in the windows that are mirrors,
you look blithely at yourself:
your very face that lost its
meaning the day memory disappeared:
that is, the day before yesterday,
or the day after tomorrow. We do
not speak. I could not care less
what happens, as you no longer know

my name. The seat once more is
vacant and occupied.
The landscape is punctuated with stairs
that press a sentence structure into it.
Your mind, like Newfoundland, is empty,
save for sand and snails,
and the small bit of sea
that the eyes are allowed to notice.
You know nothing of this all.
Your innocence is false, because
your torpid brain works feverishly
to dish out existence where there
is none, on a plate, to empty diners.

LANTERNS

As luck would have it,
the world disappears around
your throat, where the lover
clasps the moon inside
your fingers. When you
reach out to touch me,
the rivers of air collide
with skin: adhesive substance
that dives under for the
water's sake. This reveals
your great integrity.
I love you for your mottos:
the vague ideas that crystalize
inside your mind. I love
your vantage point: the
idealized perspective
in a landscape discredited
by vanity. The lanterns
burn the night away.
Fingertips collide with snow.

VARIANTS OF BROWN

Blue beams receding in the
distance like daylight, or
the humming of a fluorescent
lightbulb. The variants
of brown: leather is the
skin of cattle. Boots and
fur become a substitute
for hair, our absent woolen
covering, when winter comes.
In winter, when the body
is an insulated home, we
become mice, and in our
minds, retreat into our holes,
warm beside imaginary fires.

RISKED SOLIDITY

The dragonfly is in the bathtub.
You see through the glass, and
it ceases to be a window that
separates us, but becomes an
open space of air, a vast expanse
of carpet, like the night, through
which I crawl, my body growing
longer as the time expands.
Like sitting down in a chair
(not on, but in it), I await the
sound of your voice, daring to let
go my sense of owning any moment.
The skin grows dry, and as I
let the bones express their sense
of risked solidity, you become
a distant music, entering
my pores like vagrant light.

NEW ENGLAND BOILED DINNER

When life's pretension's stripped bare of its leaves,
and time is empty like autumn trees
that stand supine, among the barren scene
(the wint'ry air that curls about the roofs
and chimneys), smoke curls upward: hands unfurled,
whose fingers, like sharp tongues beneath the clouds
that stain the landscape like some blight that comes
upon the land, before the darkling night
descends on houses, graves, and softball fields.
The density of earth is seasoned, like
a cold meal placed atop the fire to cook:
the steam that rises from boiling water,
and scents the air with sacrificial wounds.
No answer come as yet: we wait in silence
in the room. Huddled around the fire,
we sit in expectation of the moon.

CINEMA

Am I deserving of despair?
I can feel the autumn (like
pigeons in a tree) in the air.
The leaves are oblong, and
tapered at the end, like
Japanese avant-garde cinema.
Your eyes, like light-bulbs,
flicker their filaments at me.
Do you know this?
I wonder whether, if you
could see yourself as I see you
(reflected in a mirror
at my face), you would
bounce backward, in the light of
the two-o'clock clarity
which acts as a hyphen between
morning and evening:
children playing in the park.

CAUSES

Baby eats the flowers.
Precious elephants devour
my life from my hand.
You use spontaneity
as a means of throwing
life from one place to another.
Life falls flat on its face
the way time moves around
the field. We jump,
and in our exercise
we reach a noble conclusion.
The bus descends from
the sky and picks us up
to take us across the river.
The symbology of the
metaphor is equivalent
to the inconsistency of two brothers
who are twins and have
different parents. The wind
billows through the treetops
colliding with the typewriter

that is not there, not
in the physical present.
Art becomes decorative
relative to the walls it
hangs on. Something is
caught in my throat
and keeps me from
speaking. I make believe
I do not know the words
to phrase my thoughts with.
You turn over a rock to
see the ants. I forget
to remind you that some-
thing is on the stove. It
boils over. You run in
to catch the beach-ball
as it is tossed in the
direction of your anticipated
arrival. Looking at the
clock, that is the watch
on my wrist, I tell you
that it's time to go. You
disappear through the wall.
The person reading the
account of this finds it

difficult to believe.
I do not compare you to
reality. Baby takes the knife
and peels the walls back,
saying nothing. Take the paper
and write your name, so
I know whom I am talking
about. You should emphasize
your attributes, deluding
slumber into glaring
actuality. I test your reflexes:
your knee responds. I
turn the lights off, pre-
ferring to see you in the
natural darkness of the room.
The ambiance
which emanates from you
precipitates an earthquake in
my soul. I pretend that
my emotions are translations
from the French.

WOOLLY JUMPER

The weather tears the air
into thin pieces—   looking
out the window, we see
stands of walking trees, like
peeling birches in the forest,
and feel the woods in our hair.
We forage through the wilderness
of the city that lends its life
to us the way a painter lends
his to a landscape.
The arctic nights in Greenland—
the blue hills far away
demand repeating. We lean
on our machines and watch
the stars come out into
the night-face of the sky.
You look across the road to me,
standing alone, arms at
my sides. I cannot use my hands
in the presence of your smile.
The autumnal equinox leaves us
in the throes of winter's lust.

EXERCISING SELF-CONTROL

The tables have been set,
and then you, like an unconscious earthquake,
initiate a series of tremors
through the building's basic structure
which is a metaphor for my heart,
mind, body, and soul
that permits me entrance into your being,
liquid and dismembered like a swan's
body, neck, and feathers, scattered out
over the lake in mid-winter, where
the people walk and build fires
to keep themselves warm by the portable huts
they live in as they fish through holes
they make in the ice. I wait
for you tonight in this capacity.

ASHES

You, the only remnant of the weekend,
which lies within your cloudless eye, come
quickly to the room I have left empty in my heart:
the vacant sense of what is left of self,
which you move into. Like the perception
of a room when you are in it, my effort
was unconscious. The walls slip away:
what was perceived as truth, is now discerned
as ashes, that sit quietly inside a glass container,
placed on the table to receive them.
I embark upon a dense procedure:
to relate in comprehensible terms
the vague distinctions between sensations,
returning semantics to significance.
The irony which you employ toward subtle ends
gives way to an extremity of vision,
leaving you inside this room,
behind the half-closed door with me, tonight.

MEN, LIKE TREES, WALKING

How can I think about you?
The world is far away,
and I can see it.
That's like your face,
when your hand's in
front of it: so close
your eyes can't focus.
You must move away
to see it. My eyes
begin to close, and
now that you're not
there, you are. That is,
my eyes can see you,
like a figure approaching
as the night grows dark.
The figure is barely
discernible. Men,
like trees, walking.
The transition of
the night is not
noticeable, unless

one looks away,
and then looks back;
closes the eyes, and
then opens them.
It is seen then
in stages, like a
grey scale; gradual
lineaments that
distinguish and
identify. You can-
not bear to watch
it all, to look
forever. Thank God
there is the closing of
the eyes, that cannot
take in all the world,
but some small part
of it.

PETALS

The chairs, like fields of olives without trees
stretch out across the floor, where my shoes
        run wild.
I catch in my arms the young ballerina
        in flower,
as the landscape grows like buttons
on an old man's coat.
In the meantime, you, in flower
run, scaffolding through the wilderness:
you feet, like cities; your ears,
like forest-fires;
your heart, nurturing embryos
not yet conceived.
Meanwhile, my dreams are elastic.
The shadows are cast by clothes
that hang from clotheslines
onto the wall one sees
or imagines is behind it.
A shattered lens, an exit sign
is over the door, which chooses
my memories, and yours, that may
embarrass you. But, don't worry.

I'll gather scattered petals
in my arms that move like strings
from boney shoulders: your chest,
a vacant canvass to be filled
like water glasses.
The rose behind your ear.

A LINE ACROSS THE SKY

The lack of acquiescence,
which prohibits entry into nature;
the silent milk of ocean;
the cream of life that floats on top:
a shoeshine man.
The skyline, misty in the distance:
inhuman, yet vulnerable.
A symbol of extremity,
and extraneousness:
a television that doesn't work.
An image vanished from the glass,
hidden in a grid of horizontal lines.
The vast approach of poetry,
which our conscience
plunges into: the salt
pours down our cheeks,
and falls onto the pillow.
We breathe it in like air—
The highest good, as the
Talmud notes: giving
when the donor is unknown.
The selfless explanation

that deserves companionship.
The sun going down over water.
The most extreme symbol—
not being able to enter into nature.
This places us within the realm
of the classical,
and for a moment,
we conceive of an essential unity
that is bigger than life,
bigger than both of us.
A sailboat in the midst
of nothingness.

THE DELAY OF UNDERSTANDING

The process of comprehension is complete.
You step outside the house and
breathe the air of midnight—
the air of morning that is night,
the night that is day,
the day that is the semblance of appearance.
Making a phone call from
the same phone you tried to use
a week ago, when no one was there.
A call from the street
in your neck of the woods.
A "what-you-will" of an effort
in the mid-evening, early evening,
late evening smile
that anticipates the reversal of opposites.
Here we are, another two people
who have spoken on the phone,
and, as life is a synthesis of newspaper clippings,
margarine, and poets-in-the-schools,
it is tonight that I love you most,
more than any other night.
I watch through the air for some sign of you.

You take me by surprise,
grabbing me by the throat:
the starry-eyed throat of midnight
that winks its starry eyes at you in despair.
I hope this won't offend you.
As life is a synthesis of canaries,
melons, and antelopes, I open your thighs
with my hands that are thoughts
of your thighs that are delicately carved
and smoothly polished stone
that meet my touch with melting wonder.
Life is a continual fantasy and it is real.
Pink blankets and white cats that breathe and
bear warmth and beating hearts.
Just so, so you, beneath your breast,
invite spectacular awareness of your youth.
Life is a synthesis of women's thighs,
netsuke, and whatever-you-please.
When I say that thoughts are rainbows,
I mean it.
When I say that thoughts are women's breasts
I mean that too.
When I say that the shape of things is
"carved," or smooth, or stone-like,
I mean they breathe and move, and

give warmth and real heat. And life,
the all-devouring principle of faith,
holds onto us, bringing
prophecy together with our tongues.
Let's give it a little more time.

SEAGULLS

It's the sound of his mind, thinking.
Everything is that wide; it's that quiet.
Perhaps some day we'll be able to sleep
with the door unlocked. She'll be in
bed with her own husband. The little
table in the other room, when
the voice reaches out and turns
the light off. The book has come out.
His hand reaches out. The arms are
navigating over the ocean, like seagulls.
He extends the sense of time. She has
not called; the voice reaches out, with-
out speaking. The sense of everything,
which becomes so suddenly apparent; he
cannot add a thing to it, for artifice,
or ornamental luxury, but continues,
not in spite of, but in accordance with
what gives so freely into the room:
the only context that the mind is forced
to deal with. He is there, and the moment
has become a prolongation of the same.
There, in the corner, the wall meets the

floor, and as another wall converges
at the same moment, the ceiling is
irrelevant: that is, he is not
cognizant of highth. Whereas, the
trees begin to bud, now that it is spring,
the scalp becomes dry, and the sun burns
skin. The things wait in bags, unopened.
Like stirring something in a cup, you
have lost sight of its solidity, and
along with it a sense a value in your-
self. The tea-leaves float and sink to
the bottom. A sense of potential begins
to let out air into the house, as though
a window had been opened. There is glass
between the wooden frames. An uncanny
clearness, like when the sun shines
in the afternoon, as unaffectedly as
your eye looks onto me. Hands reach out,
the fingers clutching air. Fisherfolk
let lines down from the clouds. The arms
wave, slowly, and again. You run from
the door: the trees are budding. There
is no color yet: only a sense that any
moment, the entire scene may burst
into flame. It will be you and me.

MICHAEL COOPER was born in 1952 and raised in Queens, New York by an artist father and a poet mother. Upon age 17 he ventured forth to the East Village, where he quickly became immersed in the world of the arts. He attended the High School of Music and Art and New York University, from which he received the Thomas Wolfe Memorial Poetry Award. Michael was a frequent reader at the Poetry Project and other venues, as well as being a performance artist associated with the Fluxus group. An early disciple of John Cage from age 16, he served as personal assistant to the publisher, Dick Higgins (Something Else Press), and also to the poet Jackson MacLow. Michael was also Poetry Director of the New York Avant Garde Festival, as well as serving as assistant to the director of that festival, Charlotte Moorman. He was also co-editor of EAR Magazine. He went on to earn degrees from Hunter College (B.A., magna cum laude) and Union Theological Seminary in New York (M. Div.). Michael is a retired Episcopal/Anglican priest, having served parishes with a focus on contemplative spirituality. He also had a career as a professional cellist, performing with local symphonies. He is a committed philosophical Taoist, and is the father of four children. Michael is the author of 17 books of poetry and an experimental novel, *Reap Violet Hiss*. Michael and his son live in Northeast Pennsylvania in a quiet, small town with a cat and two birds and several lovely green plants.